Mama, They Didn't Mean It

By Keesha Rivers

Mama, They Didn't Mean It

Published by Leading Through Living Community LLC

© Copyright 2016 by Keesha Rivers

For more information, contact:
IAmFlaVore Productions
c/o Keesha Rivers
PO BOX 55423
Atlanta, GA 30308

ISBN-10: 0-9891457-8-6
ISBN-13: 978-0-9891457-8-7

Dedication

I dedicate my first book to my biological mother Clara Downing-Bain. I chose the title "Mama, They Didn't Mean It" because I didn't want you to hate or hurt anyone who hurt me. In the end, it all worked out for my good. Most of those people have made peace with me, and I ask that you make peace with them as have I - in my heart. WWJD? There is nothing that we can change about it. Let's just thank God that it was not worse. I love you!

Special Acknowledgement - to My Parents

To my parents who I've always known to be Dr. Rose Rivers and Pastor Sinclair Rivers, Jr.,: you both instilled in me the love of God, set such high standards, and led by example for all of your children. You taught us that no matter what, treat people with love and kindness, and when you do that, God will bless you.

Mommy, you were a true example of a woman of virtue, always trying to find some way to help someone else, even if it required you to sacrifice your own happiness.

Daddy, you have always been a man of faith. I remember growing up in church under your leadership, always listening to your sermons which have impacted my life even through today.

From the both of you, my parents, you created an atmosphere of peace, love and teaching to be prosperous. I will forever be in your debt of love towards me and your grandson.

Special Acknowledgement - to My Son

To my dear son, Prince Brian... my heart... The one who "grew me up" in so many ways when I was just a kid myself... I LOVE YOU with all of my heart and soul. I never knew love could run so deep until I watched you grow up and fell in love with you, bit by bit, every day. You are the reason I push so hard. I am not perfect, but God made us perfect for one another.

Until I take my last breath, it will be my intention that everything I do will make you very proud of me. I have always told you that I admire you, and I have always seen the tenacity in you. I smiled every time God brought you out of a struggle because I knew you were special. You made a lot of people happy when you were born, and taught me that a mother's love for her son can never ever be replaced or broken. Brian, my dear baby boy, my pooh, my angel and my survivor...I am very proud of you and know that I will always - no matter what - have your back. Mommy loves you!

Special Thanks

To all of my fans and supporters: Thank you all so very much for believing in me my entire life. Some have come and gone, but the faithful remained loyal in spite of the trial, test, or ultimate outcome of situations throughout my life. You have also remained faithful, something that has been very rare in my life, but you always came through and made me feel special. I would like to say that I love you all and share many thanks for taking this life journey with me.

To my haters ... The word says your enemies will become foot stools, and that has ultimately come to pass. I hope that you come to realize, as I have, that you came in to my life for a reason, season and actually a lifetime, too. I realize that some trials with certain people come and remain in one's path to keep us praying. I accept that, but I must be honest, some of you have made it hard for a sister... LOL! Seriously, in the end, I have to thank you for doing your part because my faith has been tested, fortified, and ready to receive my "greater." My faith had to be tested to see if I would waiver. My faith had to be tested to see if I would faint and lose sight of my God. But through it all, I have come through, so keep the trials coming so that I may continue to prosper!

In Memory of Grandma Clara Bell

To my beloved late grandmother Clara Bell. I love you even in your death, Grandma. You died on my birthday, and I now know and understand why. You were my guardian angel - you made sure I was removed from foster care and placed with family. It was you that kept our family together and you are the reason why I was raised with my maternal side of the family. Your house was my favorite place to be when I was little, and you were the one I always enjoyed talking to most. My heart smiles at the thought of your small beady eyes and soft voice...

You loved the Lord so much, and taught me to do the same, and I will forever hold you in my heart until we meet again in heaven. One of my favorite memories of you will be when you caught some of us grandkids listening to what you called "The Blues" one night. You didn't play about your CNN News, Gospel Music and going to church faithfully. You loved the Lord and made sure we knew who He was in your life. Grandma, I miss you more than you can imagine.

To My Cuzzos

To my favorite cousins: Rhonda and Kayla. I love you ladies so very much because you accept me as I have always been. Rhonda, you have always accepted me as your blood family and I will always love you for that. Kayla, you are like a little sister to me and have always have been. We share many secrets and a bond that can never be broken, no matter what. Love you both, my sweet cousins!

Special Thanks for Divine Guidance

To my sweet *sweet* Mrs. Earnestine Lavan. Words cannot describe how much you have influenced me and positively impacted my life and that of my son. No matter what, you have always been and are still here. The love you have shown me and my son from the very beginning - since I was a teenager - has never changed. Only God could send such a vessel to us. You have seen me cry, you have felt my pain as a mother, and you have certainly marked a special space in my heart. I will always love you for loving me and my son as you have. Thank you for being you and not giving up on me, particularly in my time of need.

My Ultimate Thanks

To God, the one and only, Almighty.... This has been a long time in the making and this moment is finally here. All because You have given me the gift to write and inspire, to share my story. Sharing my life will impact others, male and female, so that they do not have to go through what I have had to endure. You made all of this happen in my life so that others may avoid feeling afraid, lonely and broken from low self-esteem. Nor will they feel frozen, unable to express how they truly feel. Thank you, God, Thank you, Father and Thank you, Lord for creating me to be a living vessel to have survived my tests and tribulations, and able to share my testimony to help someone else overcome.

Table of Contents

Chapter   Page

Chapter 1
When It All Started

A person would think that after years, or even if I must say decades, of life's lessons (some to be understood and then some not to be), that the pain would go away. I found it to be the total opposite as I grew older. I found it to be worse: my mind and my thought process, along with my trust issues, only became distorted and exaggerated, and I began to feel that I would be in pain forever, that escape was not possible.

My life began when I was eight years old (I do not remember much before then). I felt that this newly discovered life would be much better than "before"... but it was not to be because of a disturbed person. This person did things to me that a well person would not do to a little girl. I knew there was something wrong because my father did not do those things to me, no indeed, no such way! I knew "it" was not the right thing to do to a little girl because my father never read to me with my legs up in the air. I knew something was wrong... but felt powerless to say anything.

When the person asked me to read a story to him, it was odd because no one had ever asked me to do that. I was so excited to read the book, it made me feel grown up. It also made me feel less lonely because I did not have a lot of company over - my parents were really strict and limited the number and times kids could come over. So when the person knocked on the door, I opened it. He was familiar to me, and I did not even think twice about letting him in. Boy, do I regret that! I had no idea that decades later, this one act born of loneliness would so totally affect my life. I did not know decades later, it would affect my relationships and everything else that involved trusting people. The trust issues I have even now stem from that day when I was eight years old, when I was violated by that person, just because I was an innocent little girl who wanted to read a story to someone I thought I could trust.

Once I read the story to him, that person began to touch me in an unfamiliar way, down between my legs. When I looked at him, he stopped and looked me in my eyes and kept right on going. I did not know what to do at that point. I did not know if I should move, try to get away, try to fight back (but was afraid because he was bigger than me and male, so he was stronger than me). I did not know if I should or could have asked him to stop and hoped that his response would have been to honor my request. I was just a child, and had the mind of a child: I just wanted to play with my dolls and just enjoy being a child! Sadly, that was not to be, not after the molestation started - and continued...

Chapter 2
My Innocence Was Taken

As I began to remember more, year after year went by being molested, sometimes in my home and other times at his home. At one point, I began to think that it was normal. I got so use to it.

Several times I thought that I was pregnant. I remember often rubbing my stomach thinking a baby was growing inside of me, thinking that one day I may be a mom. I was too scared to tell anyone anything because I thought that no one would believe me and that the man would hurt me. Even though I grew up in a loving home, I always felt separate from everyone, or a part, for some strange reason. I always knew that I was different, ever since I was a little girl. I had visions of different things and longing to always feel a part of a family.

Maybe it was that feeling of knowing I was destined for more that gave me the courage to speak up. The day came when I set in my mind that I had had enough this person violating me, and had the guts to tell him he needed to STOP! He was shocked and looked at me with his eyes growing wide, like I had said something crazy, and he began to move back slowly. Oh, how free

I thought I was at that very moment. It felt like I had been released from a decades-long prison sentence... but it was short-lived. My attacker resumed his hateful behavior, and I also entered into another molestation war with one of his family members. This went on for a few years, both, one or the other. Finally, one moved away and ventured out on his own journey. But he would not leave me alone; he had the nerve to write me letters while he was away, living out his new career post graduation. I was shocked he had the nerve to even think of writing me after all of the pain I had gone through and still felt at the time. I began to think that he was in love or infatuated with me at an early age and did not know how to admit it since I was so young.

When asked, I would lie and say read his letters. I did not because I was scared: I thought the letters contained threats along the lines of "you'd better not say anything or I'll come back to hurt you." Every time a letter came, my stomach would twist and tighten because I did not know what to expect, and I would think that how in the world a person could - or would - be so low as to mess with a child and take her innocence without feeling bad about it. I finally got so angry and sad, I threw of those letters away. I could not believe someone would have the nerve to do what he did to me, or anyone else. After a while, the letters stopped coming and that person was gone from my life (for the most part).

He came back around years later, but when I would see him, he would look away, never spoke, and just kind of drifted off. The look on his face and his demeanor indicated that he knew something was wrong; I believe he remembered all of the torture and bad memories he brought to my childhood and many of the bad times in my life. And yet he was too much a sorry coward to even say, "I'm sorry." All he could do was try to ignore me.

As a little girl, I remember praying to God, asking that He make my attacker suffer for everything he had ever done to me: making an innocent child fearful of having a child; taking advantage of and manipulating her into reading kid stories that always ended in sex; forcing that child to pretend to be sleep in a feeble attempt to stop them from coming into her room, or in the living room to touch her "down there."

The other one who touched me...

Once the first one had finally stopped touching

me, it started again with the second one who was close to him. He would come over when he noticed my parents were not home. If I was sleep when he came over, he would touch me or try to get on top of me... or try to make me perform oral sex on him. He would not stop until he climaxed in my mouth. It felt so nasty! I felt so betrayed and *dirty*. You would think that after a period of time, he would stop, but he did not. This went on for years. I was so young, I did not know what all of "that" was about, I just knew it was not right and that "it" was not supposed to be that way.

I began to look at people with distrust and unbelief. I began to have evil thoughts of hurting people because I wanted people to feel the hurt I was feeling. I wondered why this was happening to me and if it was happening to others. I was so grateful when the assaults began to occur less frequently; I wanted to take flight like a bird with wings so I could fly far away and never look back.

I chose not to tell both my parents until I was 32 years old. Someone who had been in my life for eight years encouraged me to tell them, and I am so glad I did.

I wrote a letter and let it all out. My parents

were shocked; my mother was so hurt that she left work and had me come over to have a long talk with me. All I could do was cry. I could not stop crying. Some words my mom said to me were "Keesha, I am so sorry that you went through all of this. What makes me hurt the most is that you felt that you had to go through it alone."

My mother and I talked for hours, and all I could do was let it out. It felt so good: I was not scared anymore and I could tell someone about what happened to me. It was so much weight lifted off of my chest, I did not know how to act or what to even feel.

Chapter 3
Early School Life

There was a point when in my young life, for a few brief months that my attackers left me alone. I was overjoyed, felt safe, and was able to get my thoughts and life back together. I attended different events at school to make friends, and focused intently on my grades. It was a time that my biggest concern was what I wanted to be when I grew up.

About the same time, I realized that one of my friends had an older sibling who I knew liked me. I never said anything to him, I just focused on my friend. I went over to their house from time to time when I was bored, usually when my parents were gone, so I rode my bike. One day, my friend wanted to play directly after school (we normally went home and then I would come over later). We went over to her house, and her older brother was there. My friend's brother ordered her to get out. She left, but I was scared to move because I did not understand why he wanted his sister to leave. When my friend left the room, her brother pulled me close and started rubbing on me. I immediately pulled away and he jumped on me. He began touching me and I screamed. I screamed so loud my friend tried to open the door, but her brother had locked it. I kept screaming and yelling, but there was no use. He raped me. It seemed like it lasted a long time... I do not know how long it lasted, but I do know how I felt for years after: violated and dirty. So dirty. I never went back to my friend's house after that.

The violation did not stop when he stopped. The next day at school, my friend's brother told everyone on his sports team. I was humiliated and devastated. Now, I had to walk through the halls at school, and see and hear whispers. There was nothing I could do but watch people make fun of me. Even people who I thought were cool with me, laughed at what happened to me. Sometimes, I still have flashbacks, can still see and hear those people laughing.

I was so embarrassed I wanted to drop out of school, but something just would not let me. (I also had two parents who were not having that! They made sure we all went to school every day. Even If we missed the bus, we were going.)

It was hard going to school every day, dealing with this violation and humiliation. It weighed heavily on my heart. It made me remember all of the times I had been molested. It also made me feel like I was wearing a mask all of the time: I felt like I had to live a perfect life, pretend that nothing was wrong and nothing had ever happened, because so many people looked up to me. I was dealing with the emotional rollercoaster my life had become. "If it was not one thing, it was another" - that was what I had programmed in my mind. I was so angry; I was a kid trying to be a kid, trying to have fun, but was being forced into these adult sexual situations. All I wanted to do was have fun and enjoy my childhood years!

These violations on my physical and mental health deeply affected my self-esteem. I received many compliments from guys coming up, but they were older. And I never really thought that I was beautiful because of all of the things that happened to me growing up.

Chapter 4
Hygiene Phobia

Being raped, and the ridicule that followed, led to compulsive behavior (i.e., I am now a neat-freak and hygiene-phobic). Most of the time, all of my clothes are folded or hung by length. I feel stressed when my house is a mess; I do not like even one dish left in the sink or my bed to go unmade as I leave the house. I am very cautious of who I allow to talk around me or even whose food I eat. (Everybody's potluck may not be luck!)

Growing up, I often thought it was weird to bath or clean one's self with a wash cloth after using the restroom, but now I do those things. I have faithfully embedded those habits into my routine, weird or not - it just makes me feel so fresh, so clean. I practice these habits no matter where I am - at work or in public restrooms - and it takes me forever to refresh myself because I take the time necessary to clean my body well and treat my body right.

My mother worked a lot, so I did not really talk to her about hygiene. But I knew I had to do something, so I took it upon myself to learn the things that worked for my body. It is very important that we take the time to learn what works (and what does not work) for us, to discover things about us that no one can tell us, and to realize that no one can take better care of us than ourselves.

I do not want to make it seem that my mother was inattentive or did not care - that was not the case. She was constantly buying products for my skin (I had dry skin growing up). My most memorable moments of my mother buying products for my skin was when she came home with Avon's Skin So Soft®. She knew I loved it, so she would surprise me sometimes with a bottle of it just for me. She would smile knowing I was smiling. My mother always knew what treats to bring home.

I cannot say that I am OCD (suffer from obsessive-compulsive-disorder) because when I am tired, things are sometimes left around. I just think that over time, going through so much that made me feel dirty led to the development of my own phobia. Just the thought of not washing my hands when I get home really bothers me. After touching all of those public doors, screens, shaking hands, etcetera, gives me the "willies".

Anyone who knows me well knows that no matter what, I take my shoes off in people's houses - even if they do not. And usually, the first thing I do after eating dinner is to wash my hands, take a shower, and relax. The phrase, "Cleanliness is next to Godliness," is often used to convey respect for one's bodily temple (even though I have yet to see it in the Bible). There is so much truth in that statement, and I have learned that my temple is worth so much more than what I have been through. I became hygiene-centric when I started focusing more on me, my self-worth, and how I treated my body.

Everyone deals with being misused and taken advantage of differently. The way I have dealt with it is by developing a cleaning phobia.

Chapter 5
Courage to Share

For years, I did not respond emotionally to anyone who expressed interest in me. My mind was so focused on trying to be happy with life, I had programmed myself to push all of the pain to the back.

I have had the burning desire to write this book for decades, but was so embarrassed, confused and scared to tell my story. I put it off, waited until the "right time" and became complacent. But now it is time to tell it! I can free myself while helping someone else.

The National Negro College Fund has a saying, "A mind is a terrible thing to waste." It is true, and I will not waste my mind, or my experiences, when they can help others.

After everything I have shared, everything I had been through, you would think that was enough, right? Well, although the molestation ended, it appeared that I was "big enough" to get raped for a second time. Who would think that anyone could bare to be assaulted a second time?! Yet we are just getting started when it comes to what I have endured, and it is the reason it took me so long to write about this season in my life. It was like reliving it all over again. Painful memories I really do not want to revisit, but know that I must in order to free myself and be completely transparent in my attempts to help others know their worth.

Sometimes an older man walked by our house, and he watch me closely. He would say things to me such as "One day, I'm going to have you." Why would a man say things like that to a young girl? Although I was in my teens, I was still a young girl - I still played with my dolls. They were my make believe friends because they never talked back to me or judged me. They were pretty like I wanted to be, in every way. They had no reason to feel dirty or used...

I did not know that I should have taken what that man said as a threat to my safety, as I really had no idea what he was talking about - until the day he raped me. He had been watching my parents' pattern to determine the right time. One day, I heard a knock at the door. It was the man and he smiled at me. He then asked me to take off my clothes. I said, "What? You don't even know me." He said, "I told you I was going to have you." I was so scared... and it happened right there, at the front of the house, without another word spoken. But I remember his breathing: it was heavy, and made me think he had planned to push every breath out and onto me, almost through me. All I could think to myself was, "Here I am again in the same spot." I could not understand why anyone would want anything from me. I could not figure out what I had done that was so bad that I deserved all of this pain and abuse. All I wanted in life was to belong and fit into a family.

After he was finished, that man had the gall to smile at me. He got up, put on his clothes, opened the door and left. It made me angry, scared, and embarrassed how he left with no worries or cares in the world. He never worried that I would call the police or tell my parents. There I was, once again terrified and alone.

But everyone has a breaking point.

The Final Straw

I call this incident the last episode of my dirty feelings. My parents really never let us go outside when they were not home or at night, and this particular night was calm and beautiful. Everyone was actually home - can you believe that? My parents were in their room, my sister was in the other bed, and I was playing with my dolls in my bed. While I was playing with my dolls, I thought I heard a knock at the window. I asked myself, "Why not knock at the front door?" When I looked, it was a person I knew only in passing, not well at all.

I was also shocked because one of this man's family members had expressed interest in me through a mutual friend, so to see this man at my window left me wondering who and what gave him the idea that I had any interest in him. I did not feel endangered, so I kept talking to him, answering his questions, until I literally fell asleep with my head leaned against the window post. The next thing I remember is waking up to the man on top of me, actually inside me. I was still groggy from sleep, so I was slow to respond, but then I heard a knock at my bedroom door. I snapped awake and told the man to leave and asked him what on earth he was doing. The man left quickly and I never saw him again.

I was so angry at what that man did, I wanted to press charges against him. But I was afraid that no one would believe me because of my youth... and because the story might not make sense to anyone but me. I knew how it sounded and debated whether or not I should share this incident, but I wanted to be totally honest and transparent.

The next day, I went to school, even though I did not even want to be there. I felt like no one really loved me and hated what my life had turned in to. To this day, I have no idea what that person wanted from me or even why he decided to tap on *my* window. When we tear down others to try and fulfill whatever fantasies we have with another, that is wrong. There will always be people who take advantage of our perceived weaknesses, but we must continue to fight and accomplish what God intended us to do on this earth, no matter what. God gives us strength and the ability to go on through the process.

After that last incident, the feelings of worthlessness came back full force. I had no words and was fighting in a world to belong, but it seemed I could not win for loosing. I was so scared to tell my parents, I was slowly dying inside, and it was only a matter of time before another situation would suck me in because that is what most of my childhood had become - one big "situation."

Chapter 6
Memories & Realizations

Friendship

I remember when my childhood best friend was attacked by a group of girls that included their mother. It happened right after a tent revival service. (They say the devil gets busy as soon as you receive a blessing, and that is exactly what happened.)

It was all about a boy. One of the sisters was supposedly dating this young man, but he made it known that he liked my best friend. Interestingly, he allowed my friend to borrow his car, and we were riding around in it that night after church (showing it off - we thought were grown). Well, we rode by the girl he was supposed to be dating, and she was with her family. Needless to say, they did not like seeing us in "her man's car" one bit.

We decided to go to the store, and when we parked, one of the girl's sisters was there. An argument flared up between the sister and my best friend. They began to physically fight, and others jumped in, grossly outnumbering my friend. I was not going to let them beat her up like that, so of course I got out of the car and jumped in.

The entire time, my son was in the back of the car, sweetly sitting in his car seat. He was not even old enough to talk. That poor baby was crying his heart out, and I was not mature enough to stop and consider him in all of this, to understand that he was uncomfortable and scared in this situation. Children are very intuitive; they know what is going on, even if they articulate it, and my son knew something bad was happening outside that car.

The outcome of that fight? My best friend walked away with a scratch or two. I went to the emergency room to get stitches. By the grace of God, I did not go to jail that night and nor was my son taken away from me. I truly know that God was on my side because the police officers who came to investigate could have easily taken me away: I was disrespectful and unruly as I tried to explain what caused the fight. At the time, I could not have cared less who was wrong, from my point of view, I was a friend helping a friend. But the truth is, all of it could have been avoided if my best friend and I had not gone down the alley where the young lady lived. We knew there was the possibility of stirring up trouble, and we did it anyway. That fight could have had much more serious consequences, including me not being able to raise my baby.

Words Hurt

You know the saying "words hurt?" Well, it is true: they do. When I was in fifth grade, I remember standing in the hallway as the walls were getting painted. Our teacher told us not to put our hands on the walls. We were kids and did what kids do at 10 and 11 years old: if someone tells you not to do something, you do the opposite! I was one of "those kids", and put my hands on the wall. My teacher yelled at me, right in my face. He was so LOUD and said some really mean things, and he did it in front of everyone. I broke down and cried so hard... I walked right off campus, all the way home. My teacher did not report that I was missing. I believe it was because he knew he had said some really mean and unforgivable things.

The next day, I went to school. My teacher came over to me, looked me in the eyes and told me that he was very sorry and was wrong. Although he apologized, this was the beginning of a pattern of verbal abuse in my life. Up to that point, I had never had anyone hurl such harsh words at me, and to have experienced it coming from a teacher, in my face, in front of my entire class emotionally damaged me. The fact that he did not even call my home to ensure I had made it home safe tore me a part. Just thinking about that, even now, hurts like it happened yesterday instead of decades ago. It still hurts.

Words hurt, and that hurt can last a lifetime. Anyone who says differently is not being truthful.

Family Time

In my home, everyone had their own schedules, but my parents always made sure we all had at least one vacation together somewhere. Some of my favorite memories were from Daytona Beach, Camp Wildwood, University of Florida Band Camp, and a Church Camp in Bradenton, Florida. We had a lot of love in our home and the holidays were always very special with both of my parents cooking food that was "umm-hmm good". My mom is the baker in the family and her master's piece is a family recipe called "Milk Pie." My daddy is the cooker, and believes that everything he cooks is good... which it is!

Divine Peace

When my son Brian was about one year old, we

were going through a particularly bad time. I was a young teen mom and it was a struggle: as long as I stayed in school, I received public assistance which consisted of housing, some money, and food stamps. The guy I was dating at the time was on drugs and could not provide at all.

One "laundry day," we were trapped at the house. My car was broken down, it was raining really hard, and I had no one to call to watch my son or to take us to the Laundromat. I started not to go, but my baby did not have any clean clothes. I sucked it up, put all of our dirty clothes into a shopping cart, put a towel over Brian's head and walked to the laundry down the road in the rain. My baby did not know what was going on and he did not even cry. I was so tired, but just looking into his eyes reminded me why I was doing what I was doing - I had to push and survive for the both of us. I look back now and thank God for that time because it could have been worse. My baby sat right there so peacefully, allowing me to wash his clothes quickly and without issue.

Early Impressions

I remember watching the birth of a child. I watched the head pop out and was like "WOW!"

I was not disgusted, I was fascinated and my love for children was born when I saw that little head pop out.

I love kids and anybody who knows me knows that. Kids bring me so much joy and it breaks my heart that my innocence was taken away when I was a child. I believe that is why I am the way I am with kids. My son is my heart and when I think about him, especially when he was little, makes me want to go back to those baby days with him. We did not have much, but we had each other. I will always remember his smile and how much he hated his crib! LOL He was such a good baby and really never gave me any problems. He is my hero and I could not imagine life without him. Although he is grown, I still get emotional thinking how much he has to look forward to as an adult, and the things life will bring. I pray that God protects my baby all the days of his life, and that I should never have to bury him. Brian, mommy loves you and like I always tell you, I am very proud of you. I admire you and you will always be my Prince.

God Is With Me

God has spared me in spite of all I have endured, a life that included being molested, raped, jumped on, slapped, bullied, thrown down a ditch, scratched in the face, hit in the throat, depression, suicidal thoughts, and verbal abuse. God was in that bathroom the night I was out at the club with some friends and someone started shooting. My good friend saw me getting trampled in the crowd and pulled me up from floor so I could make it to the bathroom and to safety. I promised God if he got me out of that situation, I would not step foot back in that place, and that was my last night in that club! Someone got shot that night, but God spared my life and I have my good friend Tomalene to help me. Thank you my friend! (Smile!)

For a short time, I sold drugs to make money. I remember going off to make a run with someone I barely even knew. He could have went to jail that night. I was just going with the flow and thought that was the in thing to do: cruise around, sell drugs, dress nice, get my hair and nails done... I did not have a clue who I was or what I could (or would) become. I was confused and tried to use "that life" as a cover for my low self-esteem and pain.

I wanted to be accepted so badly that I settled into crazy situations, accepted messy relationships with men and women, and led to the selfish decision to not have any more children after my sweet Prince Brian. I just could not image bringing any more children into the world, and thought that Brian was blessed because I could not do anything about his birth since I was a minor, but really it was me who was blessed by his presence in my life.

My decisions led to so many mistakes... but that ultimately made me strong and into the woman I am today. But it was a journey. I remember coming home drunk some nights from the club, telling off police officers yet they did not take me to jail, and stopping by my parents' house before going to the club just to pay my tithes. Somewhere inside I knew what I needed to do. God was in all of "that", and although I was not wise enough to know it then, my entire experience has been part of His plan.

I was spared from death. Death:
-From dating the wrong type of guys, including one who later murdered his ex-girlfriend and put her body in the trunk of her car! The thought of that breaks my heart... that could have been me.
-From having different boyfriends who used drugs, and who could have influenced me to use drugs and suffer poor health - or death! - but God spared me: I never touched a drug and I am healthy today.

-From being raped at gun point, with my child sleeping in the next room. I was able to convince my attacker that I was willing, and after it was over, snuck out of the apartment with my son to a neighbor's house to call the police and arrest my attacker.

-From having so many different people come in and out of my life, using and taking advantage of me, including friends and boyfriends relationships, could have caused me to have a nervous breakdown. I admit I was almost there, and my parents had to travel a great distance to get me. When I got home, I slept for days. I remember my mother peeking her head into my room just to ensure I okay. I will never forget that moment.

God put people in my life who helped me, and I will never forget them. There are so many people who have been angels along my path, I pray that God blesses each and every one of them. People like

-Mrs. Lavan who loves me like a daughter and my son as her own grandson.

-Maxine Pullings who fell in love with my baby when I had to work nights and who took care of him as if he were her own.

-Honor town family, who are like my family, have my eternal gratitude.

-Jermaine Thompson, who has been a lifetime

friend, who has always supported me. In high school when I was pregnant, he would make sure I ate. Even now, he still supports everything that I do. I love you, Jermaine! -Doug, Calvin and my best friend Corrilee were brought into my life when I moved to Orlando, and I will forever be grateful to them for being my family away from family.

Revelations
I am so glad that God worked with me, building my self-esteem and showing me my worth throughout the years. Everything I have gone through, He has truly been on my side all the way. Favor is upon my life He trusts me with His people. I take the charge to lead them very seriously.

Years ago, I would not have been able to see my way anywhere near where I am today. However, have learned that everything starts with VISION. You have to see it before it even exists. When I was 16, my mother told me life is what I make it, and I never forgot it. Even when I was doing crazy things, not thinking through my actions, almost daring life to do what it willed with me, God made all things work for my good. Trust and believe that He will do the same for you. Just remember that time is a factor in everything that you do. Do not rush it; time is a part of the process.

Chapter 7
Gone Too Soon

Reshay B., My Dear Friend...

As I scroll down searching for photos to put in my first book, I came across some of my dear friend whose life was taken too soon. I miss you, my dear friend Reshay Butler. You never knew that you would live even after death, did you? Yes, you are not and will never be forgotten as long as I am here on earth. I will speak about you, about how we can love someone so much, and then the next thing we know, he is gone.

I often wonder how I will die. Sometimes I wake from a sound sleep, wondering if that is how I am to leave this world. The thought of death scares me sometimes because I do not want to be in pain when I die...

The death of my friend Reshay, who was killed when I was in high school, still hurts me all these years later. He should still be here - he had a heart of gold. I met Reshay at the boys and girls club one summer when I went with my cousins. He was playing basketball with some of other boys. His smile would make you smile right back, and it was just something about him that everyone liked. He was liked by everyone and was one of the kindest people. He understood me best of all. He and I became really close, and any chance I got, I snuck away to his house. His parents liked me and Reshay's next-to-the-oldest brother became like a brother to me. We even played Karate together! LOL It was like being a part of a family, and my big brother was Reshay.

He never tried to do anything sexual with me. He respected his girlfriend Katrina and told me one time, "Keesha, I could never be with you because of my situation. You deserve the best and I want him to treat you right. You are a very good girl." I never forgot those words throughout the years and those very same words still help me today when I feel down or betrayed by someone I truly love or have loved.

Reshay often imparted knowledge to me and encouraged me to want the best for myself. It was like he knew when I was not having a good day, and knew just what to say. He allowed me to hang around his entire family, as if I was a little sister. I could be free with him and just be myself, and when his life was taken away so suddenly, I never got a chance to say goodbye to my friend.

I was supposed to go to his house a few days before he passed away, but death came before I made it. The night Reshay died, I was awakened from my sleep by the sound of a gunshot - in my dream. I later found out that this occurred the same time that it was reported that Reshay had been shot and killed.

At first, I just thought the sound was coming from the neighborhood - that was very common to hear. Gunshots went go off like nothing, so it did not alarm me to hear it that night. It was not until later that a good friend of mine called to ask, "Did you hear the news? Reshay just got shot and killed by mistake!" I did not know what to think at that time, but I know I did not believe it. It was not until I went to school and I heard it from several other people that I realized my life would change forever.

I no longer had my friend who I called my big brother, my best and one and only friend.

I did not know so many people would be devastated by his death. The newspaper reported that it was a mistake in identity. I have never been able to live with that. My friend did not deserve to die at the age of 17. He was never able to really live! Although Reshay was young, he was wise beyond his years. I often wondered what his last thoughts and words were, what was his last reaction? Did he get a chance to accept the Lord as his savior? No one really knows how Reshay was mistaken for someone else, or who he was mistaken for. My heart still hurts for him.

My best friend impacted a lot of lives. When I decided to write about him, I reached out to find his last girlfriend. She was very nice and sweet. And it is a small world - we discovered that she is the Godmother of one of my cousins! She told me that if it was anything that I needed to know about Reshay for my book, she would be happy to help. But it was I who wanted to help her: I wanted to let her know that he was faithful to her and loved her unconditionally.

I admired Reshay and will always have him in my heart. I even said that I would name a child after him (if I had anymore), maybe a middle name. To not have my friend in my adult life has really been one of the hardest things I have ever had to deal with, especially when I am down and depressed. But even though he is not here with me in the physical sense, his words of wisdom shared so many years ago stay with me. They have helped me overcome some hard times and remind me that I deserve the best, and to never settle. It was like he was an angel on earth.

I have never stopped talking about him and have often wanted to reopen his case, not knowing if I was stepping over boundaries or not. I just want my friend, brother and angel back, and I am pretty sure a lot of other people - including his family and girlfriend Katrina - feel the same way.

I often wonder if God used Reshay to show me how a woman was supposed to be treated. Or if God was saying that good people will not stay in your life forever, so cherish them while you can. It was like God was sending me signals at an early age of how to be treated, talked to and connected to a loving family.

I kept in contact with Reshay's family years after his death. I even met up with his mother; she came over and we had girl time. She was so funny and beautiful. She always made me laugh and I adored her so. We lost touch for a few years, but a few years ago, I reached out to one of Reshay's brothers and he remembered who I was. He has a loving family now and it was so good to be in contact with a part of Reshay again. It felt like I had reunited back with my own family.

Even in death, Reshay inspires me. When I got into a bad relationship or had to go through some trial that brought me down, I could still hear his words challenging me to understand my worth. It is like a little whisper. He respected me, encouraged me to accept nothing less than the best, and allowed me to be myself. He made me know that I am priceless, and that I am not just a female, but a lady with class and I deserve the best.

Although you are not here on earth with me, Reshay, I always want you to know that I appreciate and say thank you for being a true friend to me. You made an impact on my life like no one else in such a short time as a friend. I never thought that you would be taken so soon, but you had to go. It was simply your time.

Although earth was not happy to see you go, heaven gained an angel for sure. No one can replace you friend. I still feel butterflies in my stomach when I think about that call telling me of your death - and it has been over 25 years.

I am emotional right now writing this, but it has to be told. Reshay was such a great guy to so many. I will forever hold him in my heart and he will forever be talked about with love.

Hopefully, I will make it to heaven and see him one day so we may rejoice and laugh together as we once did on earth.

I often wonder: is there really a heaven? For someone to be taken like Reshay, who had such a good spirit, I just could not understand. I miss my dear friend and I will always love him even in his death. My sweet, kind and understanding brother...

After Reshay passed away, it was like my world started falling apart. The person who had taught me so much and had made such an impact on my life was no longer there. I became angry all over again, and bitter.

Boy Trouble

It was a difficult time when I started liking boys. I was so confused, hurt, and drained by these emotions, and when added to my grief over Reshay's lost, I just simply started falling apart. I would not accept my worth and did not understand my full potential and how beautiful I was - inside and out. My friend was gone, my escape to be free from molestation, rape and abuse had left my life forever. I never thought that I was good enough or pretty enough to go on in life and was bored, so now I wanted to fill my life with things to do to keep me busy and my mind occupied.

It is sad when everyone else can tell you how beautiful you are, but you cannot see it for yourself. That started happening in my life bit by bit, and I did not know the road that it would lead to was going to be so hard. To be honest, and I can totally be free from it now by saying, I did not like myself because of everything that had happened to me. I wondered why on earth I was still here only to be abused and left feeling alone. At the time, I did not know who I was or where I was going. I only wanted to fit in and be liked and accepted, which caused me to accept things that I know I should not have from people... but it made me feel like I belonged.

Because of the schedule that my parents had with work and church, they did not know the impact Reshay made in my life. When I attended his funeral, I went by his casket and next thing I knew, I was getting help back to my seat. There were so many people there! I looked for his girlfriend to hug her, but could not find her because I could not see through my tears. I do not remember going to the grave site because I do not believe my classmate mom who took us to the funeral went there. Now that I think about it, I have no idea where he is buried and it may be best that I do not know - I do not want to see him in a grave. I am still pained from it all and it still seems so fresh to me after all of this time. I believe if he was still alive, he would have given me so much advice as a big brother. He had a sister, but her health condition led to a shortened life. I often wonder, did he think of me as a little sister as well because he never tried anything with me sexual or anything close to it. I mean *nothing ever*. We never even talked about it and I was so blessed to have such an example of a friend from where I had came from and the stuff I endured, to finally just *be*. That is all because of my dear late friend, Reshay. I felt that if he had lived, my life would have been different and I would not have settled for so much mediocrity. It was like I had given up because I was very sad and confused.

I miss my friend and I hope he can hear me from Heaven's doors. Reshay, we all love and miss you down here. Your life was worth so much to a lot of people. Another fallen solider in the war for good is gone.

Chapter 8
The Bully

As I worked through my grief over my friend's death, and my sexual abusers moved away, slowly things began to get better. About the same time, we moved around the corner from our old house, and things were very quiet. The quietness was welcomed, as it also came with peace of mind. I was also excited that for the first time, I had my own room, and I even got to pick out my own bedroom furniture. We kids even had our own bathroom in our section of the house and did not have to share it with the rest of the family. That was huge because growing up my parents always allowed others to live with us if they were in need. That meant that pretty much everything that we had, we had to share, and it was difficult sometimes.

But now, it felt so nice to be able to walk down the hall from the bedroom to the bath with just a towel wrapped around my body, verses being dressed in all of my clothes because so many people were in the house. It is interesting that even with all of those people coming in and out of the house, that none of them ever violated me, it always was from the outside.

Even when we had guests, we all operated as

one big, busy family. We were always on the go, be it to and from church, school activities, or simply hanging out with siblings and god-brothers. Our guests' friends became my family, and some great memories came from that house on Church Street.

When the house was not busy and no one was there, it was the darkest time of my life. I am still trying to decide what had become the darkest for me during my childhood memories: being violated or all of the bullying that I had endured. I never ever knew or understood why I had become such a target. Even now, I get emotional thinking about it. It feels like it all just happened yesterday, even though it has been more than twenty years.

I was bullied from middle school to high school. I do not, and never did, understand why I was so hated. It hurt because school was a safe place from all the things I had been through. Joining activities like band, chorus and different clubs allowed me to be around different people all of the time which kept my mind off of my friend's death and the abuse I had endured. I was in so many things in school, except sports, it made people wonder how I had so much time on my hands. Little did people know, that the time I spent busy with activities was an escape and place of refuge. School was a "safe haven," until the bullying started.

After everything I had been through, this was one of the hardest things to deal with and it has haunted me, and probably will for the rest of my life because I still do not understand why I was targeted.

When I was in the middle school band, we went on a trip and on our way back a boy on the bus told me he liked me, but I had no interest in him at all. He punched me in my eye for no other reason than because I was honest and stood up for myself. I got angry and hit him back. He started pounding on me like I was a man and I could not get away from him because he had boxed me into a corner on the bus seat. I could not do anything except sit there and take every punch.

After a while, someone pulled me up from the seat and the attack ended as abruptly as it began. When I got off the bus, my brothers and god-brothers were there to pick me up. When they saw my face, they were so upset and demanded to know who had done that to me. When they saw my attacker's face, my family calmed down because they realized that I had fought back.

When we got back to school, people stared at my black eye and I felt so embarrassed. But the worst part was that I got kicked out of band for standing up for myself. It hurt because band was my first love and it was not even my fault that I got into a fight. The Band Director told me that I could come back after a period of time, I believe it was to allow things to cool off, but to just kick me out of band without even hearing my side made me angry. After a while, I was invited back to the band and was able to reconnect with my band family, but it was not the same. It made me feel that every time I became attached to something or loved something, it was taken away. That realization made me angry and rebellious.

That boy who attacked me eventually apologized - to my father. He asked my dad to tell me that he was sorry. He may have meant it, but his behavior toward others and the trouble he stayed in indicated that he had not changed, and to this day, I have no idea what became of him.

In high school, the bullying was more psychological. People booed me at my very first pep rally, students walked by my locker and said, "Boo Keesha Rivers!" for no reason. I never understood why they did not liked me. I never picked on anyone, nor did I ever act like I was better than anyone or that I disliked anyone. One of the most difficult things to endure was the lack of adult intervention. At the pep rally, the staff did not say a word about any of it. I was raised to believe that adults intercede when children do not act appropriately. I was not raised to think that hating or picking on others was okay. I had always been raised to love and respect others, no matter their race or what type of person they were. My parents taught us to stand up for ourselves, but to never hate or walk around like we were better. This new world baffled me.

The day I was booed at the pep rally, I held everything in. When I got home from school, my father was home and he asked me what was wrong. I told him, "They booed me!" and on the sofa, crying my heart out. I could not stop crying and I'll never forget my father's words to me: "Keesha, you can't let them get the best of you. You got to keep going because that is how life is, you got to keep moving. People talk about me all the time and you just got to keep moving."

Those words my daddy spoke to me have helped me through difficult situations since.

Every time I get down and out, I hear my dad's words and I realize I have to just keep going. There is always going to be something or someone in life who we may not agree with or someone who will set us off, but that is just life and we got to keep pushing to reach our destiny.

My first year of cheerleading I could not do a toe touch. All of the other cheerleaders knew how, and they laughed at me. I pushed through anyway, and determined to do well. I was very committed - on time to every game, giving it all I had, and (I thought) proved myself, thereby becoming part of a the cheer-family. The truth came out in year two. When it was time to try out, we had a series of rehearsals. I skipped one to help a friend - he had just broken up with his girlfriend and needed a shoulder to cry on. When it came time for tryouts, I did a great job, but they did not pick me for the main squad - they told me that I could be an alternate. When asked why - it was because I had missed that one rehearsal. I could not believe it! I was mad, but took the alternate spot. But then they called me back, saying that one of the girls they had chosen quit, so I could now be on the main squad. I felt betrayed, used, and humiliated. I was so angry, I quit the team.

Looking back, I wish I had stuck with the cheer squad. Even back then, I often thought it would have been nice to stay and be counted as one of the prettiest preppy girls in school. Where I come from, if you were African American and you made it to the cheerleading team, it was a privilege - there were only two or three of us invited. But I was young, and had been through so much pain, I allowed my emotions to get the best of me. I quit something I had truly loved and wanted to be a part of because of the mean actions of a few.

It was hard going day by day knowing I would be bullied, but not sure how. I knew I would because I had become a master at projecting apathy. The more I heard people talking about me, calling me a "black Dolly Pardon," or saying that I "wanna be a white girl," the more I portrayed boredom. People picked on me for what I wore, because my mom was always at school, and my parents worked a variety of side jobs to make ends meet, and my father was a preacher, and simply because my mom was not home taking care of us because she worked hard as a nurse. (If it was not for my father trying to balance everything with the entire family, I truly do not know where we would all be.)

The bullying had gotten so bad that I did not want to be around my own race. I tried to hang out with other races since it seemed my own race was against me. I never understood why my race would call each other the "N" word and then expect for others to respect them. My bottled up anger from abuse found something to latch on - rage against fellow African Americans. Gratefully, that did not last. God changed my heart through an incident at school. One day, I was walking down the school halls and this girl who everyone feared starting picking on me. She was so mean, you could not even look at her without her getting upset. When she saw me, she began to pick on me and out of nowhere, this girl who I barely knew, got in a fight with her... for me. A black girl, who I did not know, stood up for me because it was the right thing to do. She was suspended... for me. That selfless act changed my heart so quickly my head spun. I was so touched, overjoyed that someone liked me, cared enough about me, and thought enough of me to stand up for me. She was not even my friend - we were not even acquainted. She was simply someone who I knew from the neighborhood, who had taken it upon herself to stand up for something she saw was wrong. Her name was Sabrina, and I considered her another Angel from God who was sent to help me and teach me another lesson along the way: not to hate but to continue to love in spite of what people say and to be proud to be black.

The bullying was so bad that a student hit me on the bus and the bus driver did not even say anything, and even my family members who were on that bus did not try to help me. It was like they enjoyed watching me be abused.

There was this one time a so called friend from the neighborhood was supposed to have my back in a fight (someone thought I liked her boyfriend and I tried to show my tough side). It happened in the bathroom. I went to hit the girl, she ducked and started hitting me over and over. After she hit me several times, she left the bathroom with her friends. I walked out, hurting and embarrassed. Later, I went back to the bathroom where my "friend" was supposed to be, and saw her there - laughing with other girls about the fight. That scarred me for life. I did not have many friends, and to have my closest neighborhood friend hide from and then laugh at the fight, broke me down and I lost trust in friends.

The bullying did not stop, so I realized I needed to get tough - so I did. I started standing up for myself: when kids started yelling, I yelled back;

when they wanted to fight, I fought back. I had so much anger in me that I quickly learned that I needed to be careful of my strength - one time, I almost gave a girl a concussion on the water foundation at school pounding her head over and over until a classmate pinned me on the ground to stop me.

Although I felt relieved that people picked on me less and less, and was happy in my new-found confidence and courage; there was also a part of me that was say and hurt that I had to defend myself that way because deep down, I truly did not want to hurt anymore. I only did all this because I did not want to be bullied anymore. All I wanted was to be accepted, to be part of a family. I did not understand why I had to fight to feel like that.

Fighting for survival became routine, and sometimes there would be no rhyme or reason for it. One day, a person I had not seen in years attacked me as soon as I walked through the front door of a mutual acquaintance's home - in front of a group of people! I was shocked because not only did I not do anything to that person, but the people in the room did nothing to stop it. The person hit me and threw me around the room, with no explanation as to why. Years later, I confronted that person about it, and they did not even remember. He told me he was sorry and had no clue as to why he did it. Crazy, but it is along the same lines as another incident that left me speechless: someone asked me to drink his pee. Yes, absolutely disgusting! I was so young, I had no idea what that could even do to a person. I was stunned and totally caught me so off guard, but to that person, it was normal - he asked someone close to me to do the same thing.

It saddens me that people can take advantage of others innocence and think nothing of it. I am the person I am today because of the times people have tried to - or succeed in - taking advantage of me. In my mind, my world was a battle that required me to always be on my guard and/or ready to fight. I just wanted to belong, to be loved, that is all.

Although bullying was a huge part of my childhood and school experience, I have forgiven and even connected via Facebook with some of the people who bullied me. They have grown and changed, and have been there to help me in business as well as my personal life. I thank God for how He bought those people back in to my life, to teach me forgiveness. It is so much better to forgive and let go because if I had not forgiven, they would not have had a chance to bless me on my journey.

In talking with some of the people who bullied or disliked me, they were very honest in telling me that it was simply jealousy at the root of their behavior. Others told me that they did not know why they disliked me. I believe not knowing is a cop-out, and indicates they still have some growing to do so they may be honest with themselves; or they are fighting generational curses that have yet to be broken.

These discussions have taught me that when dealing with certain folks, as believers in Christ we must forgive and accept that 1) they do not mean what they are doing, 2) they are not where we are, and 3) the same God who delivers us from our struggles can do the same for them. We must pray for these people because we all need prayer, and have or had some type of struggle where we needed others to pray for us.

Chapter 9
High School Light

Of all of the disappointments in my life and in particular my high school years, God clearly had His hand on me the entire time I was going through each trial. When I was pregnant with my son, I moved away to stay with a family member in another city, I dropped out of school and was about to give my son up for adoption. Thankfully, God brought me back to my senses. Once I returned back home, all of my teachers allowed me to make up my work and I graduated on time.

I will always be thankful to all of my school mentors who made school life a safe haven for me. When I began to get involved in activities and the bullying began, after Sabrina fought that girl for me, no one else said a mumbling word to me. I later found out that when I moved away I was actually missed!

My mentors through the years were remarkable. Mrs. Keating was the first to recognize my talent as an eight year old singing in the school chorus. I did not even know I could sing, I just wanted to be involved, to feel that I was a part of something. In middle school, I was again in chorus, this time with

Mrs. Adams. Everybody loved and adored her so much - she made singing fun! And in high school, it was my Band Director "Mr. C", who is a legend in my eyes. Everybody knows him and he is well respected. He made such a positive difference in my life. There was this one time I was mad about something that happened during a football game and Mr. C sat me down the entire night. I was so hurt, but I deserved it because as a leader at that time learning how to develop those crucial skills, I should not have allowed that situation to get the best of me, and especially not in front of everyone. Now that I look back at it, I am so glad he did that. It taught me to accept that everything is not going to be peaches and cream all of the time, that as a leader, I had to learn self control and to move forward because others are depending on me to do what I am supposed to do. That doing so is true leadership by example.

I am also very grateful to Mrs. Yma H, my Girl Scout troop leader, as she was a very positive influence, and Mrs. Vera Riley, my favorite childhood teacher.

In high school, I was invited to be a part of a singing group called 2nd Episode and I guess you can say was we were leaders. It was fun and we had to be examples in school and in the community. We sang at Senior events, an Art Festival in the community, and even had rehearsals at my home in the front room. I also loved going to Honor Town, visiting often. Those were some of my happiest times, singing and having friends. I did not really have many friends in school so the singing group was special. It was all African American females, so I was excited that my own people asked me to be a part of something phenomenal - in spite of the "white girl" and "Dolly Pardon" comments. We were always at each other's homes and became good friends. I became very close to Satoya - we were like sisters. Satoya lived down the road and we did everything together. We even lived together at one point as we got older, and she kept my son for me when I had to work. Satoya left an imprint in my heart as one of my favorite friends growing up. We may not have always seen eye to eye, but she was there for me in more ways than one when it came to my son. We used to have so much fun everywhere we went, and it got to the point that everyone in our city knew that if you saw one of us, the other was close by. I will always have love for Satoya because she showed love to not only me, but to my son as well. She sacrificed her time to watch over my son when she did not even have kids of her own. She quickly became Auntie Toya to Brian.

Chapter 10
First Love

During what was supposed to be the most exciting years of my life - my teens - I had one battle after another. One battle occurred during a summer that changed my life forever. At the time, it felt like an answered prayer, something I had been waiting for all of my life (or so it seemed). I had been longing to simply fit in and feel important, having both parents home rather than working and going to church all of the time. I was in high school band camp and saw these good looking boys walk into school. I had not seen them on campus before and heard others mumbling and talking about getting a closer look. Some ventured to the front office to see who these guys were. Well, following the crowd, I went along, too. The boys were registering for school. They were with an older woman who appeared to be their mother or relative. We were all looking, pointing and smiling at them. There was one I stared at more than others, and I caught him looking at me, too. He had long eye lashes and when I saw him smile, I smiled. I guess at that time, I was being what the ol' school saints would call being "fast." He was light skinned, had "nice" hair, and long eyes. I wanted to know more about him: who he was and where he had came from, and why he wanted to come to our school.

That young man made my heart drop. I was so serious about him that I worked my parents so he could come visit me. He was the very first boy my parents actually allowed to come a visit me at the house. This guy was not like Reshay, where I would catch rides to go see him like a little sister missing her brother. This boy became my first boyfriend.

I was smitten. He got my number and I was shocked when he actually called because I really did not think that I was worth calling. After all I had been through, it was so sweet that he took the time to call me, to want to see what I was about and who I was. While we were getting to know each other, we stayed up all times of night talking on the phone. And during the day, his auntie or dad picked us up from school and we went back to his house so we could hang out. It seemed like I was always having dinner at his house, with his entire family, and I loved playing with his little sisters before they went to bed. His extended family (aunts, cousins and grandmother) became a part of my father's church, and we attended church together. It was like being a part of a real family. I even sang at some of his aunts' weddings and my father baptized most of his family when they moved down from Philly. We were in love and we were always together. But that was soon to end.

One day, I was in the library and some guy was trying to flirt with me. I did not know it at the time, but my boyfriend's brother saw it, and told my boyfriend. The next thing I knew, my boyfriend came up to me, upset that I did not tell him about the flirtation and before you knew it, he had confronted the boy and broke his nose!

My boyfriend was expelled from school, and later went to Job Corps to finish high school. I was devastated that we were not able to be together all the time anymore, and shocked because no one other than Sabrina had stood up for me. I did not know whether to be happy or sad: my first real love was kicked out of school defending me.

It was hard adjusting to his absence. No longer would we walk each other to class, talk on the phone all night, see each other before each class and be together after my school activities. He was the first guy to penetrate me with love, an emotion that did not leave me feeling dirty or scarred; it left me feeling that I finally mattered in someone's life. I felt like a queen, not a dirty little secret.

It was an amazing time in my life... and a lie tore it completely a part. A lie that even today, I do not know the truth. As adults, we talked about it, but we agreed that it was in the past, and things turned out the way they were meant to be.

We broke up, but we did remained friends throughout the years. We would check in with each other on and off, and when we completely lost touch, I would from time to time ask his family how he was doing. Although we were not long in love, he was and is forever in my heart, and that left a mark that no one else. We call passing notes in school and talking on the phone "puppy love", but this love had my heart completely and left a print like no other.

We always remember our first, no matter who it is or how it felt. However, it is even more intense when you feel that your first will always be in your life because you never want the feeling to go. It hurt me so bad when we broke up, I did not even know how to handle the pain. When I heard he had moved on, my heart was broken. When I found out that he started dating a girl who had the same first initial as me and gave her initial ring he brought me for

Christmas, my anger ignited, and I politely went to her house and got it. I felt violated worse than when I had been physically attacked, that someone I had loved had given something that was meant for me to someone of little consequence. I did not care that we were no longer together, that was my ring. No one had never brought me anything like that before so it did not matter that he had moved on, I had not. I kept that ring for years before I finally let it - and the anger - go.

Twenty years later, he found me and we rebuilt our friendship. We apologized to each other for all that had passed between us, and I told him that I appreciated him making me feel like I mattered in his life. We put the past where it belonged - behind us - and we are continuing to build up each other up moving forward.

That was one of the best seasons of my life and I will always remember my first love and my sweet family from Philly!

Chapter 11
Teen Mom

After my first love ended, I got a part-time job, trying to stay busy. I also wanted to follow in my sister Angel's footsteps since she was working, too. I admired Angel for being so independent at such a young age, and I wanted to feel the same way. One day while I was at work, I saw this popular guy from school. Everybody was crazy about him because he was so good in sports. Of course I did not think he was interested in me (I did not think he even knew I was alive), so I did not speak to him when came in or passed by the store - even though he came every day. However, one day I got enough nerve to speak to him. He smiled and asked me how I knew him. I told him that everyone knew him. He smiled and kept going.

He shocked me one day when he came in to the store and gave me a piece of paper with his number on it. I asked him what I was supposed to do with it and he said read it and call me. Growing up in my time, I was always taught to have the boy call you, so when he instructed me to call him, I waited a few days trying to play hard and then eventually I did call. He instantly knew who I was and we built a friendship from there. Later, it turned into a closer friendship and he even taught me how to drive. He loved me so much. I knew he did because when I told him I was pregnant (it was not his child), he just wanted to be there with and support me.

I was not with my son's father very long, and I wanted my son to be named something very special, something to symbolize the importance of growing into a fine young man. I decided to name my son after someone who I felt was with me for me and would support me no matter what, so I named my son Brian after this great guy. I had fallen for him, but was never really in love with him like he loved me. Not because of anything he did, but because I still did not know my own worth. I kept thinking, "How could I be in love with him when he was not the father of my child?"

Eventually, I called our budding romance off and it devastated him. I knew he was going to hurt, but I had no idea he would still be effected years later. We stayed in contact and sometimes he floated the idea of us getting back together, trying to see how I felt about it. But I was guilty: I felt like I had let him down by not being honest about still having feelings for my first love and not too long after, the sticky situation with my son's father. How could I stay in a relationship with someone who gave so selflessly, when I knew I did not feel as strongly as he did? It was the right thing to do even looking back on it because I know how it feels to be betrayed and used, and I did not want to do that to him.

My mind was so messed up from all of the past hurt, it was sad that I could not see or appreciate love with him. My feelings were strong enough to be in a relationship with him, however, my heart was still hurting from the past. I did not know my worth, so I could not see the worthy individual in front of me, who wanted to build a life with me. It is true that "hurt people, hurt people." I know God was pleased with my decision, and I was relieved that I had made the best choice for both of us. I could have married him, but it would not have been fair to either of us. I was taught to honor marriage. What I had seen from my parents' marriage was so deep and connected that I chose to get out before things got out of hand. I will always have love for him knowing he truly loved me.

For a while after that, I remained single. I did not want to continue to be hurt and continue to hurt others, but my good intentions did not last. I was still trying to fill the void of loneliness and trying to fit in. One after another, my next relationships were disasters.

I dated guys who sold drugs, guys who did drugs, and guys who physically abused me. I was in relationship with a guy for over a year who tormented me unceasingly. One time he kicked me down into ditch in the road and beat me until I screamed for my life. No help came, but he ran because of my screams. Another time, we were arguing in the car and he started going over 100 miles an hour. I yelled and cried, begging him to please slow down because my son was in the car. He slowed the car down, I got out of the car and before I could get my son, the guy kicked me into (another) ditch and drove off. I almost lost my mind! I walked aimlessly for some time. The guy eventually came back to get me, and the craziness continued.

He stole my food stamps, stole my car, and left my child - who was a toddler at the time - home alone while I was in class. That last one led to a huge fight, and I kicked him out. Unfortunately, I let him back in, and we went back to our cycle of violence. I tried to leave: I moved out and went to live in a hotel, but he found me. Sometimes he left me with no money or would steal it, making it hard for me to buy groceries. My son lived off of white potatoes, TV dinners and his juice. I made the same meals over and over all the time, but I sucked it up because I determined that as long as my son had food to eat, I would be okay. I tried my best to make sure he was safe in that horrible situation. I just did not know my worth.

It still haunts me that a person could do all of that to another human being, especially when a child is watching. And I beat myself up wondering how I could allow such people to violate me that way? How could I think so low of myself, as if I just did not care what happened to me?

My son was the answer to all of my prayers. He is my guardian angel baby and my life. My son, who I almost put up for adoption because I was so young and wanted to finish school and go on to experience college life; my son, who by the grace of God was born when I was a minor and could not have an abortion; my son, for whom I wanted the best, so for almost a decade I remained single. I moved to Orlando with someone to start a better life for us, and after that did not work out, I decided I had come too far for anymore foolishness. Every person after that, got it hard core and I meant every word and action.

After a while, I started building my confidence, and I purchased a home after a while. Brian was in school, we were eating better, and I started working and making friends. Life was beginning to pick up for us and I started feeling safe. I did not want to move back home because I felt like if I did that, I would not have survived or my son would have been in danger.

I will always appreciate my son's father for blessing me with my Prince. Once I realized I would be a single mother, I decided not to weep about it and to get our future started. Years later, Brian's father reached out to him, and he was able to meet all of his other siblings. It was such a wonderful day and time for my son. I never wanted him to feel that I kept him from his father or his siblings. I could be mad about a lot of things in that situation, but I reasoned why get mad and stay mad when it was not in God's plan for all of us to be together? It was in God's will for me to have my son and my oath to God was to raise him right.

I tried very hard to be a good single parent and would not give anything for it. I will not speak negatively or harbor bad feelings towards my son's father because if it were not for our time together, our son would have been conceived. I have never understood why people bash their children's other parent because it did not work out. It did not work out and that is that.

I would be lying if I said that I was not bitter for a time, but over the years God healed me of that by showing me His power and His plan for us. My son has loving siblings and is loved by his other side of the family. The rest is in God's hands, and it is my job to be his mother and guide him to truth, which is knowing Christ Jesus. Yes, it hurt me to see my son hurt about different things that happened along the way, but that will be part of his testimony. It is not my place to interfere in what God has ordained. We must forgive, accept and trust the Lord's work completely in every situation, leaning not to our own understanding. Show love and kindness to all with no malicious intent and God will honor His word every time.

So with that being said, in all things and at all costs, I thank God for my son's father. Without him, there would be no Brian, who is my Prince. I always taught my son that love is a two way street - it goes both ways. I also taught him not hold anything in his heart against anyone because no one is perfect - including him. Someone had to forgive us for our wronging, so we must continue to forgive and move on.

I also taught my son to always check in with both sides of his family, and not to wait to see who calls first. This teaches us to do right no matter who does - or does not - respond because God wants us to show our love and kindness no matter what. If we do not continue to teach our kids these things, they will be hurt trying to manipulate people into loving them.

My son was always taught to love in spite of other's behavior because God first loved us. His father always wanted him to have his last name so that if anything ever happened to him, Brian would be taken care of. That was enough for me and I honored his wishes. Regardless of any feelings or any episodes or events that take place between the parents, there should never be a situation where one parent does not have any say so in the matter of the children.

My son's father was there financially (which is better than most), but I could never be a father to my son. Raising a young African American male required mentors, so God brought wonderful men into Brian's life who did just that. Although I wish my son's father had been more physically present and involved, Brian never heard me speak negatively about his father and never will. Children one day have to grow up and comprehend things on their own.

Chapter 12
The Adoption I Already Knew About

I will never forget when my parents called me in to their room and told me I was adopted. My father spoke first while my mother just looked at me. I will never forget that look and the words that were spoken. But before they told me, I already knew. A lady at the neighborhood store told me she knew my birth family. She told me I looked just like my birth mother. I was kind of confused (I look just like both my birth and adopted mothers), but then I immediately put two and two together: the woman I was told was my birth mom was not.

So this explained why my biological mother came to visit me so often, did my hair, even stayed the night sometimes and gave me money. Once I found out the truth, I hated to watch her leave. I was a part of her and I wanted her to be a part of me. She would say, "I'll be back," but I still cried in my room, wondering why I could not go with her.

Later on, my birth mom wrote me a 10 page letter explaining why she could not keep me. She said she was so young and was going through so much. She tried to keep me, but she was in a rough place in her life and wanted what was best for me. I truly thank the Lord for allowing her to feel that someone in our family would be the best fit. And she was. My mother always encouraged me, telling me that I was smart and that she admired me. She never held me back from my dreams and was always supportive in whatever endeavor I tried. She taught me to support and love who you care for and just allow a person to be themselves because one day, they will have the opportunity to become successful.

Although the woman who raised me was my family by blood, she is my mother because she chose to raise me as her own. We did not really talk about who my biological father was because it really did not matter. The father whose last name I proudly carry is my family, and I could not have asked for a better daddy. My father and I have so many fond memories together. He picked out my prom dress, he kept my son when I was finishing my classes, and he knew me inside-out. Some of the fondest times with my father was when he, my sister Angel and I drove to Frogs (a local store) in his old green "Sanford & Son" truck.

I was raised in a Christian environment. My parents never cursed in front of their children, never fought in front of us and never took sides.

However, there was still a void, a feeling of something missing and a desperate desire to belong. I could never explain that void, I just knew coming up that I felt incomplete and I never really understood why. I think it was because I realized that I would never have the chance to be raised with my maternal side of the family with both biological parents with the experience of siblings running around yelling and screaming at each other. I always wanted to feel like I knew both sides of my family. I tried to hide it, but could not because it always bothered me, especially during the lowest moments in my life when I felt down and depressed.

I often wondered would it have been better or worse to have been raised by my biological mother? Would I have loved visiting my Cousin Connie's house when I was little, just to get away from it all? Would I have loved staying at my Grandma Clarabell's house during the summer and experience the longing of wanting to go home at the end? Would I have gone straight to college and not gotten pregnant in high school? Would I have been interested in guys that sold drugs, did drugs or wanted multiple women at a time? Would I have avoided dating men who abused me, trying to fill the void to be loved? I wonder...

Chapter 13 Knowing My Worth
The Next Chapter of My Life

No one is perfect. We all need forgiveness to be forgiven. I had a rough childhood, but that was no excuse for me doing wrong. I used to lie and I even stole one time - candy from a store (I got caught doing it, so my career as a thief was short-lived, thank God).

I lied over stupid stuff, just to try to fit in. I used to lie about where I was from: I would tell people I was from New York because I thought it was the popular thing to do, and it was deemed boring and poor to be from a small town like I was. It seemed like lying could get you what you wanted when you were little. It only got me a bad reputation and no one wanted to trust me. I had to prove myself constantly when I started learning my worth and wanted to show the world the person I had become.

People do not realize life experiences greatly impact their decisions, and is a big reason people act the way they do. I am not making excuses, but there is a reason some people lie, steal, cheat, and behave badly. It is because they do not realize their own worth. I have learned that my worth is more valuable than anything that I could ever purchase, or obtain as a gift. It is the reason I work constantly to better myself. If we do not learn our worth, then how can we teach anyone else to respect or love their own?

My mother taught me that life is what I make it, and she was certainly right about that. She and my father always tried to include me in anything the other kids had going on just to make me feel a part of the family. All I ever wanted was to feel included, but did not realize what I wanted had always been right in front of my face. I always wondered what it would be like to have both my parents, not realizing that I DID have both parents - God had indeed answered my prayers.

I have siblings, both adopted and biological. I know all of them and we call each other brother and sister. At the end of the day, we all have a bond and that is being family. I love both of my mothers and my father who raised me. I even love the people who bullied and hurt me. I had to learn to love them, and I did through the love of Christ, because I wanted forgiveness and I had to forgive to be forgiven.

Throughout all of my wrongdoings, God

provided me with grace and mercy to carry me through and forgive me as well. No one gets a pass and we have to work hard for what we want to get what we want later. We can never stop learning and surrounding ourselves with positive people who know and can help us do more than we can do by ourselves. We should forever be pursing, learning, helping others and growing. Our lives should never just be about us and what we can get out of it. We should be a blessing when we do not even feel like being a blessing because it may be a test right before we receive our next blessing. I am sharing all of these things because these are lessons that I would like to pass on to others to them know their worth.

Thank you all for loving me enough to take to read this book. I can finally say that this process of sharing and embracing my past has freed me from past hurt and relieved my mind of the weight in carrying it all. When I decided to tell my parents everything, they both wanted to know why I felt I had to carry all of this and not say a word. It is because I love them and did not want to hurt them.

Now that I am an adult, I realize we should never have to go through anything alone. For there is a season that will come when not even your own thoughts will be able to hide what is in your heart. Your heart will only speak truth so now, the next step is to allow your heart to heal so that you can help someone else. I am rooting for you! And Mama Cookie, this is why I never wanted you to worry... They simply did not mean it. Some people just are not loved and nor are they given a chance to be raised with love as I was. Those people's lives are full of generational curses and other demonic displays. I was so blessed through it all because it made me who I am today. You made the best decision for me and I will always love you for that. Mama, they did not mean it. Mama, please I ask you to forgive them as I have forgive them. In the words of our Savior "they knew not what they" did. If they had, they would never have done it. They did not mean it.

MY EARLY YEARS

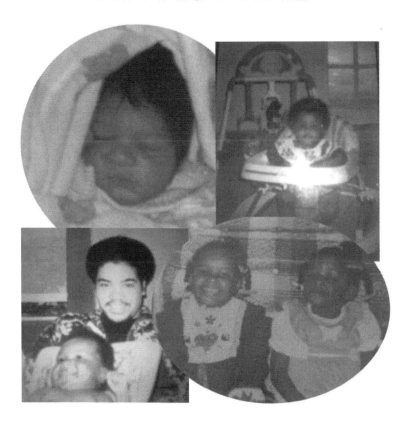

TIMES OF CELEBRATION

IT'S ALL ABOUT FAMILY

GOD HAS TRULY
BLESSED ME

About the Author

Keesha Rivers is the founder and CEO of many ventures that include Fla'Vore Productions, K.R. Consulting, and The Fla'Vore-Aide Radio Show. She is also the author of Mama, They Didn't Mean It, a successful real estate investor, plus-size model, and highly-sought after motivational speaker and life coach.

Keesha enjoys her success, but never forgets where she came from. Although she now resides in Atlanta, Keesha comes from humble beginnings. She was born of a teen mother in Virginia, adopted and raised by her aunt and uncle in Central Florida, and overcame many trials to become the person she is today. Those challenges include being abused, molested, and bullied; feeling isolated and depressed; struggling through failed relationships and teen motherhood; and juggling college, motherhood, and employment. Through it all, Keesha has maintained her faith that God was with her, and she shares her incredible capacity to forgive and its positive impact on her success with all who will listen.

"Know your worth" is one of Keesha's favorite sayings, as it led to her success as an entrepreneur, finding fulfilling and loving relationships, and being the best mother she could be to her son Prince Brian. She mentors children, young adults and business clients on a regular basis, along with providing Life Coaching skills to all ages.

Always seeking ways to expand her knowledge and skills, Keesha accepted the challenge to serve as the first Pageant Director for former Ebony Magazine Commentator Jada Collins. She so enjoyed the experience that she founded her own fashion show exposition and inspirational-entertainment showcase for the up and coming models, artists and vendors. In addition to her book, Keesha also writes inspirational comedy sketches and parodies.

Keesha obtained her Bachelor of Science degree in Psychology and Masters Degree in Business Management. She is a member of the National Congress of Black Women, is a domestic violence and anti-bullying advocate, and community activist who has made it her mission to stand up for youth. That passion has led to her working alongside other great activists that include Martin Luther King III, Bernice King, Roland Martin and Rev. Jessie Jackson; and also being a guest on the Samy Priso Show on the Bright House Channel 49, several magazine interviews, working with the Wordnet, attending President Barack Obama's second term inauguration at the invitation of Congresswoman Corrine Brown, and attending Florida State Senator Geraldine Thompson's swearing-in ceremony at her personal invitation. In April 2013, Keesha became the youngest honoree ever to receive the Central Florida "Living Legends Oscar Award" for her community work and achievements.

"If we are not becoming an advocate for someone else, then our works are not enough. It's not the works that reward you, but the sacrifice for someone else is what will keep you successful." *Keesha Rivers*

Learn more about Keesha at www.IAmFlavore.com.

Made in the USA
Middletown, DE
07 November 2021